CONTINENTS UNCOVERED

SOUTH AMERICA

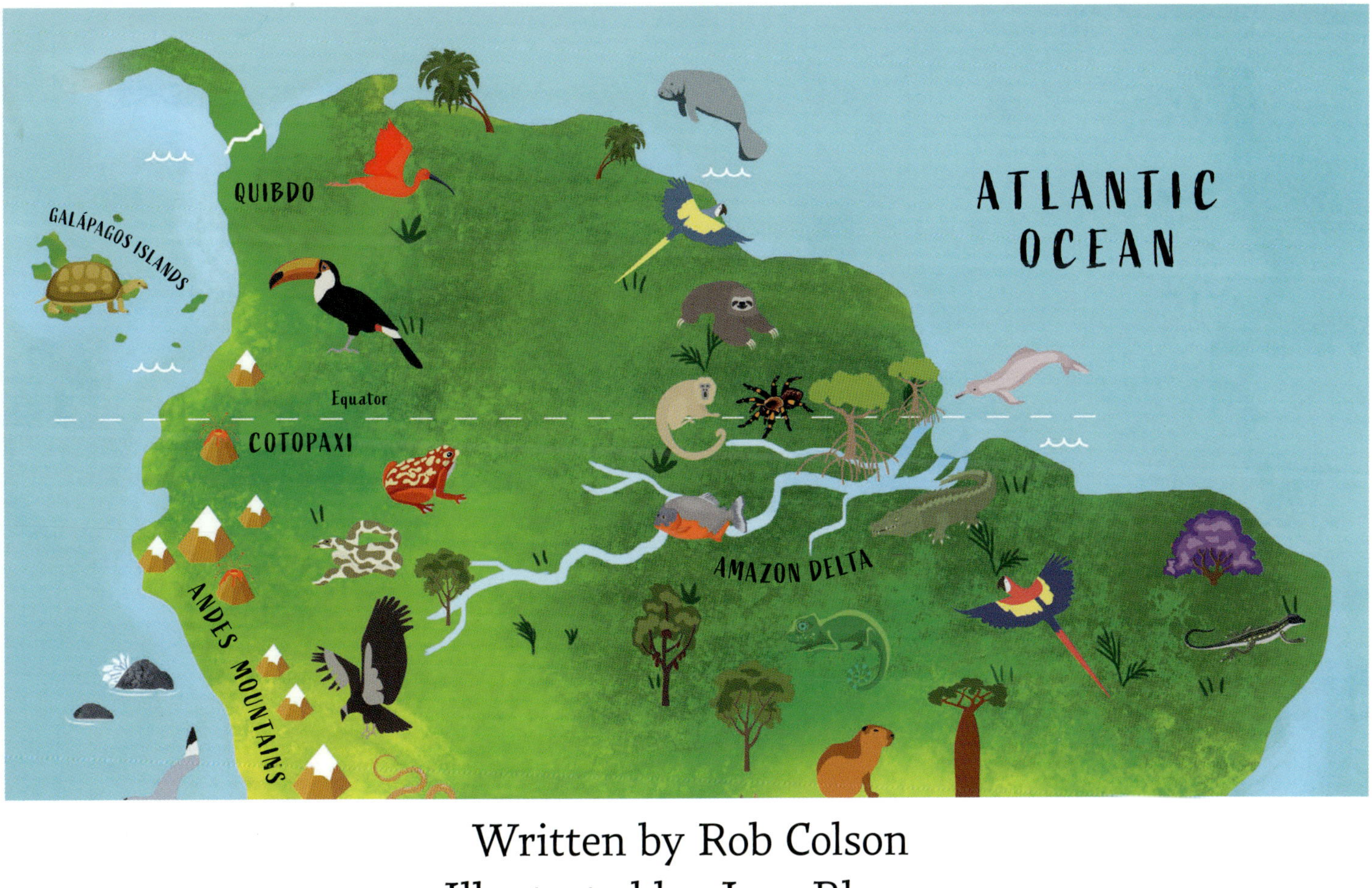

Written by Rob Colson
Illustrated by Josy Bloggs

Enslow PUBLISHING

Published in 2025 by Enslow Publishing, LLC
2544 Clinton Street
Buffalo, NY 14224

First published in Great Britain in 2023 by Hodder & Stoughton

Series Editor: Amy Pimperton
Series Designer: Ed Simkins
Illustrator: Josy Bloggs
Map illustrator: Amy Zhing

Manufactured in the United States of America

CPSIA compliance information: Batch #CSENS25: For further information contact Enslow Publishing LLC, New York, New York at 1-800-398-2504.

Please visit our website, www.enslowpublishing.com. For a free color catalog of all our high-quality books, call toll free 1-800-398-2504 or fax 1-877-980-4454.

Cataloging-in-Publication Data

Names: Colson, Rob, author. | Bloggs, Josy, illustrator.
Title: South America / by Rob Colson, illustrated by Josy Bloggs.
Description: Buffalo, NY : Enslow Publishing, 2025. | Series: Continents uncovered | Includes glossary and index.
Identifiers: ISBN 9781978539198 (pbk.) | ISBN 9781978539204 (library bound) | ISBN 9781978539211 (ebook)
Subjects: LCSH: South America--Juvenile literature.
Classification: LCC F2208.5 C657 2025 | DDC 980--dc23

We recommend adult supervision at all times while doing the activities in this book. Always be aware that craft materials may contain allergens, so check the packaging for allergens if there is a risk of an allergic reaction. Anyone with a known allergy must avoid these.

- Wear an apron and cover surfaces.
- Tie back long hair.
- Ask an adult for help with cutting and glueing.
- Check materials for allergens.

CONTENTS

WHERE IN THE WORLD?

South America is the fourth-largest continent in the world. Sitting entirely in the Western Hemisphere, it stretches from just north of the equator to the subantarctic zone. It is connected to North America by a narrow isthmus to the north. Just under half of the continent's land area and population are found in the largest country, Brazil (see page 27).

POLITICAL MAP

PHYSICAL MAP

MAKING MAPS

Mapmakers create different maps to show different types of information. Political maps, such as the one to the far left, show human features like countries. Physical maps show the geographical features of a region and use colors to show features like habitats, rainfall, or altitude. For example, in the physical map to the left, high ground is shown in brown or yellow, while low ground is colored green.

HABITATS

A habitat is an area that is home to a particular group of plants and animals. The habitats of South America vary enormously. The lush Amazon Rainforest (1) teems with many different kinds of life. By contrast, in the forbidding Atacama Desert (2), only the toughest animals and plants can survive the dry conditions. Herd animals range across the open grasslands of the Pampas (3), while the creatures that live in the Andes Mountains (4) need to be sure-footed and nimble to negotiate the steep mountain slopes.

FACTS

- Area: 6.8 million miles (17.8 million square kilometers)
- Major rivers: Amazon, Río de la Plata, Orinoco, Paraná, São Francisco, Rio Negro, Tocantins
- Highest peak: Aconcagua, Andes Mountains, Argentina, 22,837 feet (6,961 meters)
- Major mountain ranges: Andes Mountains, Sierra Nevada de Santa Marta, Serra do Mar, Mantiqueira Mountains, Wilhelmina Mountains

SOUTH AMERICA

South America is home to an incredibly diverse range of plants and animals. This is the result of its varying habitats, which include thick rainforest to the north, vast grasslands to the south, and rugged mountain areas to the west.

JAGUAR

The jaguar is the largest cat in the Americas. It can survive in a wide range of habitats, including open grasslands and wetlands, but it is most at home in dense forests. The jaguar is an excellent climber and spends much of its time in trees. It hunts large mammals, such as the giant anteater, marsh deer, and capybara.

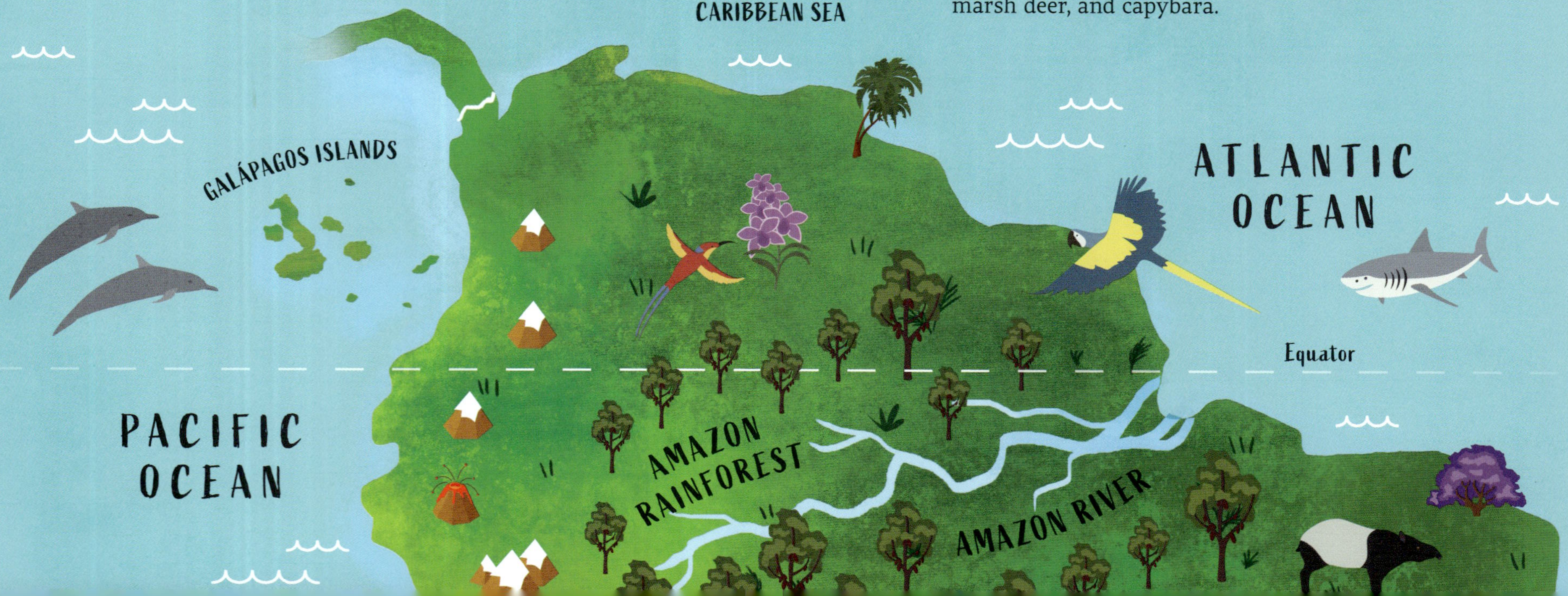

GRASSLAND

Grasslands extend over areas that receive too little rainfall for trees to grow. Grasslands are found in most parts of South America, occupying about one-eighth of the land. Around the Andes Mountains are high grasslands called the páramo, sandwiched between lowland forests and snow-capped peaks. In the south, the Patagonian grasslands dominate the chilly plains and plateaus. Many of South America's grasslands have been converted into farmland.

RAINFOREST

Tropical rainforests are woodlands that experience heavy rainfall all year round. They contain the most diverse range of life found anywhere on land. More than half of the world's rainforest area is found in South America in the form of the Amazon Rainforest. It is made up of nearly 400 billion trees.

AMAZON RAINFOREST

The Amazon Rainforest is the largest tropical rainforest in the world. It extends across nine different countries. Winding through the heart of the forest flows the mighty Amazon River, which is more than 6 miles (10 km) wide along much of its length.

FACTS

- More than 20 percent of all the river water in the world is found in the Amazon River. Its headwaters start in the Andes Mountains in Peru. From there, the water flows 4,000 miles (6,400 km) to the east to enter the Atlantic Ocean.

- The piranha is a small predator with a powerful bite. This fish usually hunts on its own, but occasionally hundreds of piranhas will come together to take down large prey, such as a capybara.

ACTIVITY

Make a blowgun

The people of the Amazon Rainforest sometimes hunt small animals using blowguns. Make your own blowgun and use it to fire marshmallows!

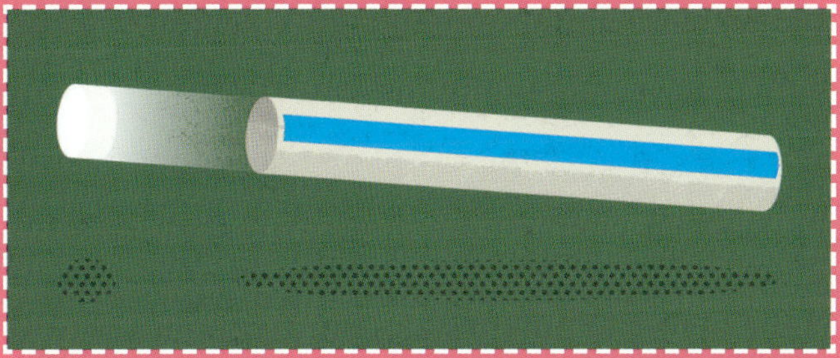

1. Take a piece of stiff paper and roll it into a tube along the long side so that it fits snugly around the circumference of a marshmallow. Tape the tube in place.

2. Roll the marshmallow in some flour and insert it in one end of the blowgun. Hold the same end to your mouth and blow as hard as you can! How far can you get the marshmallow to go?

AMAZON RIVER DOLPHIN

The Amazon river dolphin finds its way around the murky waters of the Amazon River using echolocation. It gives off rapid clicks and listens for the echoes that bounce back off nearby objects.

PAMPAS

The Pampas is a vast plain extending across Argentina, Uruguay, and southern Brazil. There are few trees, and the landscape is dominated by grassland. The soil is very fertile, and much of the Pampas has been turned into farmland.

FACTS

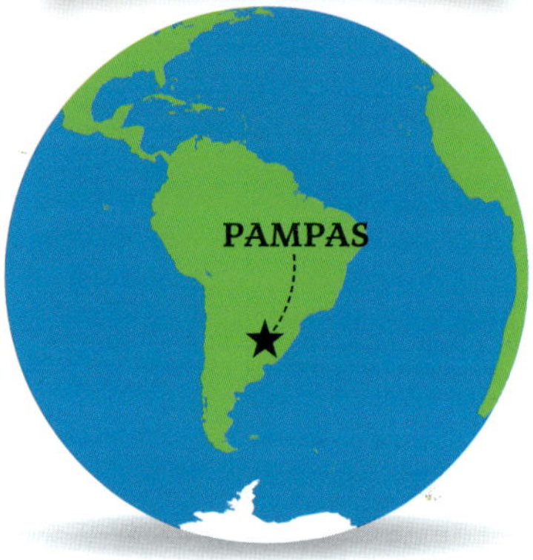

- Weighing up to 175 pounds (80 kilograms), the capybara is the largest rodent in the world. It lives in large groups around rivers and lakes, feeding on grass and aquatic plants.

- Gauchos are cattle herders on the Pampas who are renowned for their horse-riding skills.

RHEA

The rhea is the largest bird in South America, at more than 3 feet (1 m) tall. It cannot fly, but it can run at up to 37 miles (60 km) per hour. The female rhea lays up to 10 eggs in a nest. She then leaves the male to look after the eggs, while she looks for another male to mate with.

ACTIVITY

Tie a Honda knot

Gauchos use lassos to catch cows. Try your hand at tying a Honda knot, which gauchos use to make their lassos.

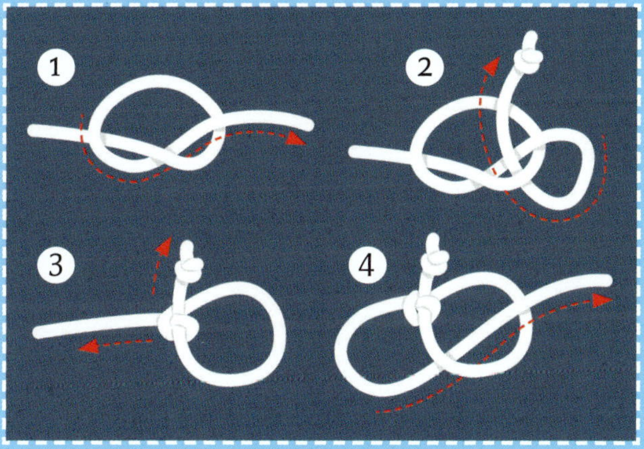

1. Tie a loose "overhand" knot near the end of the rope.

2. Tie a tight overhand knot at the very end of the rope and pass the end through one side of the loose overhand loop.

3. Tighten the loose overhand knot. This creates a circular Honda knot.

4. Feed the other end of the rope through the Honda knot to make your lasso.

UNCOVERING THE NORTH

The tropical forests in the north of South America cover an area that is warm and wet. The western side of South America is dominated by the mighty Andes Mountains. Snow falls on the peaks of high mountains, even near the equator. Many rivers flow from the highlands to the coasts, creating large valleys as they go.

COTOPAXI

Cotopaxi is an active volcano in the Andes Mountains. An almost perfect dome shape, it stands 19,393 feet (5,911 m) high. The volcano has erupted more than 50 times since 1738. Major eruptions result in mudslides called lahars, which can travel more than 60 miles (100 km). Lahars are created by the sudden melting of the ice around the summit by hot lava.

WET AND DRY

WETTEST PLACE:
QUIBDO, COLOMBIA, 354 INCHES (8,990 MILLIMETERS) OF RAIN PER YEAR

DRIEST PLACE:
ATACAMA DESERT, CHILE, 0.5 INCH (15 MILLIMETERS) OF RAIN PER YEAR

AMAZON DELTA

The Amazon Delta in northeast Brazil is the place where the Amazon River joins with the Tocantins River to drain into the Atlantic Ocean. As it enters the delta, the mouth of the river is 205 miles (330 km) wide. The water drops huge amounts of sediment around the delta, creating wetlands in which mangrove forests grow. Mangroves are trees that thrive in salty water.

IGUAZÚ FALLS

Straddling the border between Argentina and Brazil, the Iguazú Falls are spectacular waterfalls that mark the boundary between the Upper and Lower Iguazú Rivers. A chain of 250 separate waterfalls extends for 1.6 miles (2.7 km), making it the widest falls in the world. The highest falls are 270 feet (82 m) high.

ATACAMA DESERT

Extending along the west coast of South America, the Atacama Desert is one of the driest places on Earth. In some parts of the desert, no rainfall has been recorded in modern times. Only a few tough plants and animals can survive in these extreme conditions.

FACTS

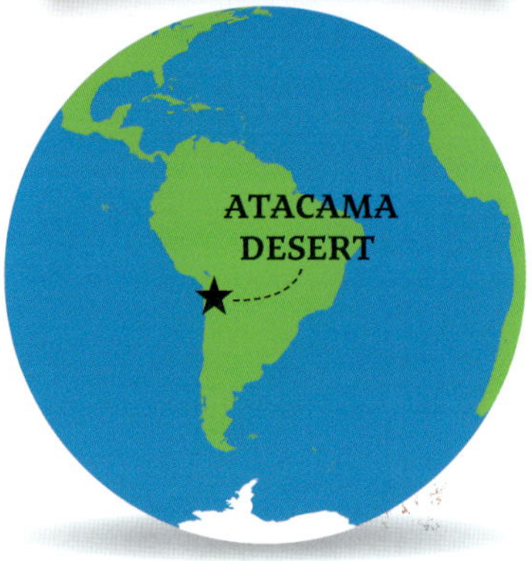

- The Atacama Desert is the world's oldest desert. Some parts of it may have been dry for 200 million years.

- Although it rarely rains, a fog called the Camanchaca often forms around mountains in the Atacama. The fog provides enough moisture for plants, such as lichens and cacti, to grow.

CHILEAN FLAMINGOS

Chilean flamingos live in huge flocks around salt lagoons. They wade through the water, feeding on brine shrimp and algae. Flamingos are born a pale gray color. As they grow up, their feathers turn pink due to bacteria in their food.

ACTIVITY

Fog in a Jar

Fogs, such as the Camanchaca, form when water vapor in the air condenses to form droplets of liquid water. With the help of an adult, watch this happen inside a jar.

1. Ask an adult to fill a jar with very hot water and leave it for about a minute.

2. Pour away most of the water, then place a bag filled with ice cubes over the top of the jar. Watch as a fog forms. Hot air rises and cools inside the jar. As the air cools, the water vapor in the air becomes liquid, creating a fog.

LAKE TITICACA

Lake Titicaca is the largest lake in South America. Surrounded by snowcapped peaks, the lake straddles the border between Peru and Bolivia, high in the Andes Mountains.

FACTS

- The surface of the lake is 12,500 feet (3,812 m) above sea level, making it the highest deep lake in the world. It has an average depth of 330 feet (100 m), making it safe for large ships.

- On the tiny Isla de la Luna (Island of the Moon) are the remains of an ancient Inca nunnery. According to Inca mythology, the god Viracocha commanded the moon to rise from the island.

TEXTILE ART

The people who live around Lake Titicaca are famed for their textile art, using the skills of the Inca people who lived there before Europeans arrived. Fabrics are woven together using looms.

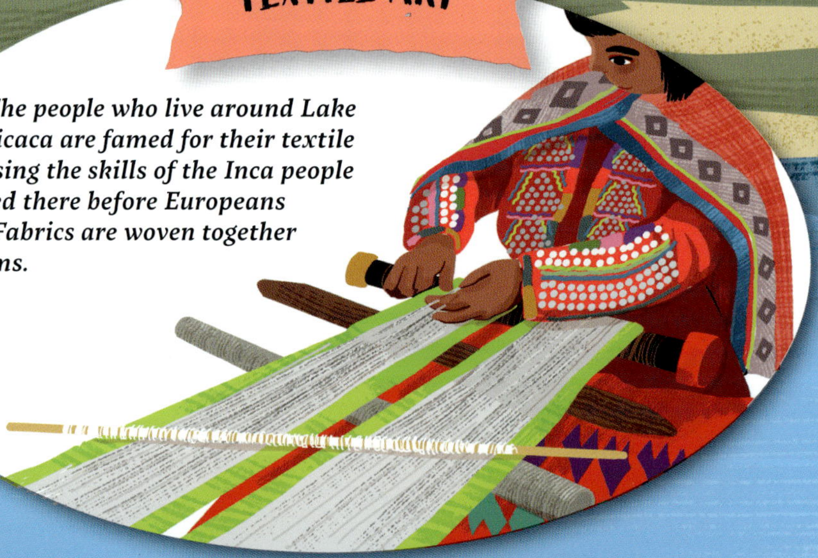

ACTIVITY

Make a baby turtle

Try your hand at textile art and weave a baby turtle.

1. Paint three craft sticks green and ask an adult to help you to glue them together in a star shape, as shown. You can draw on a head and feet with a black marker.

2. Wrap a long piece of yarn a couple of times around the center. Now start weaving using the "God's eye" pattern. Wrap the yarn once around one craft stick, then once around the neighboring craft stick, and so on. When you want to change color, tie on a new piece of yarn. When you are finished, tie the last piece of yarn to the very first piece.

GALÁPAGOS ISLANDS

The Galápagos are a group of volcanic islands in the Pacific Ocean about 620 miles (1,000 km) from mainland South America. They are part of Ecuador. Many kinds of rare wildlife are unique to these remote islands.

FACTS

- Although the islands are on the equator, the water around them is very cold. Strong currents bring cold water up from the Antarctic.

- Giant tortoises are found on seven of the islands. These huge reptiles move very slowly. They can live for nearly 200 years!

MARINE IGUANAS

The marine iguana is the only lizard in the world that swims in the ocean. The iguanas gather on rocks to warm themselves in the sun before plunging into the cold water to feed on algae. Marine iguanas are found only on the Galápagos Islands, and they vary in color from island to island.

ACTIVITY

Darwin's finches

In the 1830s, the English scientist Charles Darwin visited the Galápagos Islands. Darwin studied the many kinds of finches found on the islands. He discovered that each species of finch had a differently shaped beak depending on the food it ate. These are three of Darwin's finches and their preferred food.

Large ground finch
Large, short beak for cracking hard nuts.

Medium ground finch
Small, short beak for eating soft seeds.

Green warbler-finch
Long, sharp beak for spearing insects.

Study the birds where you live. What do their beaks look like? What food do you think they like to eat?

UNCOVERING THE SOUTH

Along the western coast of South America runs one of the hottest deserts on Earth, the Atacama. In the south, it is much cooler, while the upland areas experience cold mountain conditions. At Cape Horn, on the southern tip of the continent, icebergs from Antarctica float close to the shore.

PACIFIC OCEAN

ELQUI VALLEY

The Elqui Valley is located on the southern edge of the Atacama Desert. The region is famous for its vineyards. Its sunny climate, steep slopes, and fertile soil make it an excellent place to grow grapes. The Elqui Valley is also an ideal location to stargaze. The clear skies attract astronomers from all over the world to study the night sky.

MOUNT FITZ ROY

Mount Fitz Roy in Patagonia is a mountain on the border between Argentina and Chile. It stands 11,171 feet (3,405 m) high. Although not the highest mountain in South America, Mount Fitz Roy is considered to be the hardest to climb. Each year, the best climbers in the world come to Mount Fitz Roy to test their skills on its steep, windswept slopes.

HIGHS & LOWS

HIGHEST POINT:
ACONCAGUA, 22,838 FEET (6,961 M) ABOVE SEA LEVEL

LOWEST POINT:
LAGUNA DEL CARBÓN, 344 FEET (105 M) BELOW SEA LEVEL

RÍO DE LA PLATA

The Río de la Plata, or River Plate, is a wide bay that forms part of the border between Argentina and Uruguay. There are several small islands in the Río de la Plata. The islands are slowly growing over time as the passing water deposits sediment around them.

THE ANDES MOUNTAINS

The Andes are the longest mountain range in the world, forming a continuous chain of highlands along the west of South America. They are also the highest mountain range outside Asia, with more than 100 peaks over 19,500 feet (6,000 m) high.

FACTS

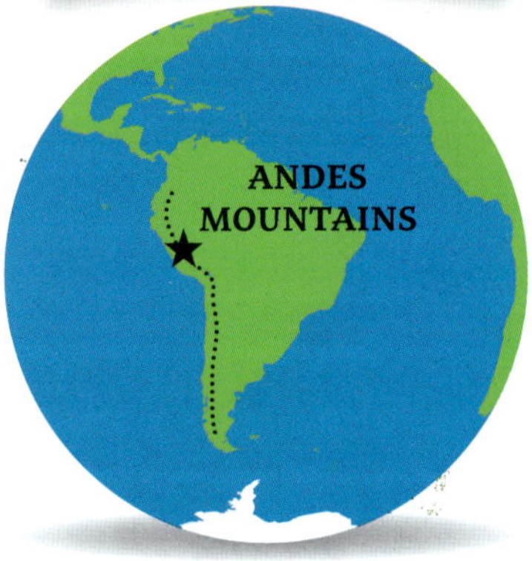

- The Andes stretch 4,350 miles (7,000 km) north to south along the west of South America. They span seven different countries.

- Many of the mountains in the Andes are volcanic. The mountain Ojos del Salado on the Argentina–Chile border is the highest active volcano in the world, standing at 22,615 feet (6,893 m).

ANDEAN CONDOR

With a wingspan of more than 10 feet (3 m), the Andean condor is the largest bird of prey in the world. It is a scavenger, which means that it feeds mostly on dead animals. The birds may travel more than 125 miles (200 km) per day in search of food.

SPECTACLED BEAR

ACTIVITY

Straw pan pipes

People of the Andes play an instrument called the pan pipes. Make your own pan pipes from straws.

1. Take five wide straws and, with the help of an adult, cut them down to different lengths: for instance, 7 inches, 6 inches, 5 inches, 4 inches, and 3 inches (16, 14, 12, 10, and 8 cm).

2. Cut two identical rectangular pieces of cardboard, about 6 inches (15 cm) long and 1 inch (2.5 cm) wide. Lay a strip of double-sided tape along one piece of cardboard and stick the straws to it as shown so that the ends are aligned on one end. Then place double-sided tape along the other piece of cardboard and stick it to the other side.

3. Blow across the tops of the straws to make sounds.

TIERRA DEL FUEGO NATIONAL PARK

Tierra del Fuego is an archipelago (island chain) on the southern tip of South America, shared by the countries of Chile and Argentina. Its rugged landscape features mountains, glaciers, and waterfalls. The island is constantly battered by winds and storms, so the plants and animals that live there need to be tough!

BEECH TREE

FACTS

- The lower slopes of the mountains on Tierra del Fuego are covered with a subantarctic forest, featuring many species of beech tree. Above 1,970 feet (600 m), the trees are replaced by small bushes and grasses.

- The name Tierra del Fuego means "Land of Fire" and was given to the area by the first European explorers who saw the many bonfires of local people as they sailed past.

ROCK SHAG

The rock shag, or Magellanic cormorant, is an expert diver. It can reach depths of 33 feet (10 m) or more during its dives to the seafloor in search of food. Rock shags nest on ledges on rocky cliffs.

ACTIVITY

Make a diver

Diving birds make their bodies more dense so that they can descend through the water. This "diver" does the same thing. When a bubble of air trapped inside it is squeezed, the "diver" becomes denser and sinks.

1. Place a pea-sized piece of modeling clay around the end of the point on a pen cap, as shown. This will be your diver.

2. With the help of an adult, fill a 1-liter plastic bottle with water. Carefully place the pen cap in the bottle, clay end down. It should just float at the top. If it sinks, remove some of the modeling clay and try again.

3. Screw the cap on the bottle. Squeeze the bottle at the side and watch your diver sink. Release the pressure, and the diver rises again.

PEOPLE AND PLACES

South America has a population of 420 million people. The most widely spoken languages are Spanish and Portuguese. Many South Americans have a mix of European and indigenous heritage, while others are descended from enslaved Africans who were brought to South America between the sixteenth and nineteenth centuries. South America's unique cultures reflect the rich mix of these diverse groups.

COLOMBIA

Colombia is the only country in South America with a coastline on both the Pacific Ocean and the Atlantic Ocean. The country spans a wide range of climates, from the cool capital city of Bogotá, high in the Andes Mountains, to the sweltering resorts on the northern Caribbean coast. The official language is Spanish, but 68 other languages are recognized, including more than 60 languages of indigenous peoples.

MACHU PICCHU

High on a mountain ridge in the Peruvian Andes sit the ruins of the ancient city of Machu Picchu. The city was built for the Inca emperor Pachacuti in about 1450, but it was abandoned a century later. Before the Spanish arrived in the 16th century, the west of South America was dominated by the Inca Empire. The Inca built a network of roads connecting different parts of their empire across the Andes Mountains.

BRAZIL

Brazil is the largest country in South America. Most Brazilians have a mix of European and African ancestry and speak Portuguese. About 1 million indigenous people live in Amazonia, speaking their own languages. Brazil's largest cities are São Paulo and Rio de Janeiro. Every February, Rio holds the world's largest street carnival, in which brightly dressed dancers and samba bands parade through the streets.

BRAZIL

AREA: 3.2 MILLION MILES (8.5 MILLION SQ KM)

POPULATION: 220 MILLION

MAIN LANGUAGE: PORTUGUESE

CAPITAL CITY: BRASÍLIA

LA PAZ

At more than 11,483 feet (3,500 m) above sea level, La Paz in Bolivia is the world's highest capital city. The city is 42 miles (68 km) southeast of Lake Titicaca, in a canyon through the Andes Mountains. Most of the people of Bolivia have a mixed Spanish and indigenous ancestry. In addition to Spanish, many indigenous languages are spoken, including Quechua and Aymara.

CHILE

Chile is a long country that spans most of South America's Pacific coastline. Nearly half of the country's population lives in or near the capital city, Santiago. Chile has been described as "a country of poets'," and two Chilean writers, Gabriela Mistral and Pablo Neruda, have won the Nobel Prize for Literature.

CHILE

AREA: 293,437 SQUARE MILES (760,00 SQUARE KM)

POPULATION: 19 MILLION

MAIN LANGUAGE: SPANISH

CAPITAL CITY: SANTIAGO

PEOPLE AND PLACES

The three countries in the southern half of South America are collectively known as the Southern Cone. Spanish is their main language, but Argentina, Uruguay, and Chile have influences from many different European countries. All three countries share a love of soccer and a strong barbecue tradition, reflecting the extensive cattle ranches that cover much of the land.

MONTEVIDEO

The capital city of Uruguay, Montevideo, sits opposite Argentina's capital Buenos Aires on the north side of the Río de la Plata (see page 21). With a vibrant cultural life and a growing high-tech business sector, the city has been voted the best place to live in South America. Its high quality of life attracts people to live and work there from all over the world.

ARGENTINA

AREA: 1 MILLION SQUARE MILES (2.8 MILLION SQ KM)

POPULATION: 45 MILLION

MAIN LANGUAGE: SPANISH

CAPITAL CITY: BUENOS AIRES

ARGENTINA

Argentina is the second-largest country in South America. The official language is Spanish, but most Argentinians have some Italian ancestry, and the country maintains close links with Italy. The capital city, Buenos Aires, is famed for its vibrant nightlife. Buenos Aires is the home of the tango, a slow and intense dance that started among poor communities on the outskirts of the city.

QUIZ

1. In which country is South America's highest mountain located?

2. Across how many countries does the Amazon Rainforest extend ?

3. By what name are cattle herders on the Pampas known?

4. Chilean flamingos turn pink as they grow up. What color are they when they hatch?

5. What is the name of the group of islands where marine iguanas live?

6. Which desert is the driest place in South America?

7. The Río de la Plata forms part of the border between which two countries?

8. The largest bird of prey in the world lives in the Andes Mountains. What is its name?

9. What is the name of the southernmost tip of South America?

10. What is the main language spoken in Brazil?

11. The world's highest capital city, La Paz, is found in which country?

12. Which country spans most of South America's Pacific coastline?

Answers:

1. Argentina **2.** Nine **3.** Gauchos **4.** Pale gray
5. Galápagos Islands **6.** Atacama Desert **7.** Uruguay and Argentina
8. Andean condor **9.** Cape Horn **10.** Portuguese **11.** Bolivia **12.** Chile

GLOSSARY

Aquatic plant
A plant that grows in water, either rooted in the mud or floating freely.

Canyon
A deep, narrow valley with steep sides, usually with a river flowing through it.

Delta
A flat, fan-shaped area of land created where a river splits into many different branches and deposits sediment.

Echolocation
A way of locating objects around you by bouncing sounds off the objects and listening for the echoes. Many species of dolphins and bats use echolocation to find prey.

Equator
An imaginary line around Earth that is the same distance from both the North and South Poles. The equator divides the planet into the Northern Hemisphere and the Southern Hemisphere.

Habitat
An area with the right conditions for a particular set of plants, animals, and other living things to live. Those conditions may include soil type, rainfall, or temperature.

Indigenous peoples
Also known as First Nations or Aboriginal Peoples, groups who were living in a region before it was colonized by people from another place.

Isthmus
A narrow strip of land that connects two much larger areas of land.

Lagoon
A shallow body of salt water that is separated from the ocean by a narrow strip of land.

Plateau
(Plural: plateaus) An area of high, flat ground.

Rainforest
A dense forest rich in life that grows in areas with plentiful rainfall all year round.

Sediment
Small fragments of solid material, such as silt, sand, and gravel, that are transported by rivers and deposited in a new location downstream.

Species
A group of closely related living things that reproduce with one another.

Strait
A narrow stretch of water that connects two seas or oceans.

INDEX